*Where
The
Forest
Once
Stood*

Praise for Where The Forest Once Stood...

"A thoughtful and timely collection of poems. Contemplative, funny, urgent and hopeful, these varied and vibrant poems form a cohesive whole, united in theme and narrative, as Hare explores the natural world and our responsibility to protect it."

- Guy Bass

"Clever, inventive and entertaining"

- Louis de Bernières

"Anyone who thinks they are too small to make a difference has never met a honey bee" - *anon*

WHERE THE FOREST ONCE STOOD

Copyright © Julie Hare 2024

Julie Hare has asserted her right under the Copyright, Designs and Patents Act, 1988, to be identified as the author of this work.

All rights reserved. This book or any portion thereof may not be reproduced, lent, hired, circulated or used in any manner whatsoever without the express written permission of the author.

Printed in the United Kingdom

First printed 2025

A CIP catalogue record for this book is available from the British Library.

ISBN: 978-1-0683955-0-5

For Ian, Darlie and Oran

With heartfelt thanks to Katherine Smith for reading my poetry and saying the words 'I think you should write a book' and then for actually making it happen. Thanks also to the ever-patient author Matt Beighton for lending his expertise and bringing the book together so beautifully.

Contents

There's a fast-food shop where the forest once stood..................1

Dear Mother Earth..................2

The Cub..................3

14 4

Cuttlefish 5

Geese 6

Ads 7

The Bee 8

Dear Mohammed, ...10

Kennings — Land 11

Kennings — Sea 12

Kennings — Sky 13

When you're done, love, just throw it away..................14

Bowerbird 15

Nearly A Limerick..................16

The Flight of the Last Bee 17

Dear Mother Earth, ...18

Life is sweet as a peach on the beach..................19

The Pangolin 20

Chameleons 22

To the hedgehog in my garden 23

The Heavy Hippopotamus 25

The Crooked Crocodile 26

The Worrisome Worm 27

The Ghastly Ghost Bat 28

Dear Mohammed, ...29

A Symbiosis Love Song 30

Snakes 31

Earth Warrior	32
Animal Snacks	34
Nature Bop	35
Plunder the ocean	36
Lessons from mellivora capensis	37
Dear Mother Earth,	38
Haikus	39
The Crab Apple Tree	40
Questions for a whale	42
Questions for an albatross	42
Sprinklings of blue where no blue normally grew	43
The Egg	44
The Sinking of the Ark	45
Collective Spell	46
Fish	47
Dear Mohammed,	48
Strangler Fig	49
Annual General Meeting of Global Wildlife Representatives	50
Tankas	52
A Rainbow of Life	53
Blackout Poetry — Step 1	54
Blackout Poetry — Step 2	55
Blackout Poetry — Step 3	56
The Assassin	57
The Sea	58
A Naturalist's Bookshelf	59
Dear Mother Earth,	60
How to infuriate a literary tiger	62
Take heart, grasp hope: you are mightier than you know	63
Weather	64
A little bird told me	65

Volcano	66
Along came Mungomery	67
Verae Peculya Names	69
The answer is trees	71
You are welcome here	72
Where the Poems Go	73
Responsibility: A Reverse Poem	74
Dear Mohammed,	75
Keep Connected	76

There's a fast-food shop where the forest once stood

There's a fast-food shop where the forest once stood,
With a plastic counter made to look like wood.

The oak which saw nine hundred springs,
Which sheltered 13th century kings,

Unearthed by those with an appetite,
For a quick, carbon-heavy, unwholesome bite.

There's a fast-food shop where the forest once stood,
With a plastic counter made to look like wood.

The roots which held the forest in place,
Now shrivelled and revealing tunnels of space,

So, the unstable ground no longer holds tight,
Floods again and again—an ominous blight,

There's a fast-food shop where the forest once stood,
With a plastic counter made to look like wood.

Gone the cool, lush world of the undergrowth,
The natural respite from the sun's fierce glow,

And in the act of tearing this up,
Man released more carbon into the ozone's cup,

Now children sit here, inside they squeeze,
Rows of grey, chewing faces fiddle with polymer trees.

There's a fast-food shop where the forest once stood,
With a plastic counter made to look like wood.

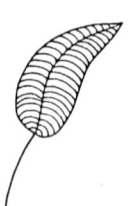

Dear Mother Earth

Dear Mother Earth,

I have a pet worm,
I found him in the park,
And took him home in my pocket,
With mud and leaves and bark.
I put him in an empty fish tank,
With a netted lid — to stop the cat.
I've called him Splat.

But my sister says he is gross,
That he is slimy, creepy and vile,
She says, 'Bugs are for stepping on!'
She said, 'Just you wait a while.'

I know he's just a worm,
But he's my harmless friend, too,
I don't know what to do.

From Mohammed
Aged 6 (nearly 7)

The Cub

The cub stretches,
Paws push deep
Into soft leaf-littered earth
And bottom raises,
Tail rigid.
Completing the perfect 45-degree angle
With the ground,
A mouse disturbed,
Dashes in desperate endeavor
Over mountainous tree roots
Towards sheltered safety.
The cub's nose twitches
And her eyes narrow,
Sharpening her focus
On this escapee,
This fugitive.
A whimper-warning from mum
Ignored,
And the cub is off,
Racing towards
The slender, slim, snaking tail
Which brushes audibly
Against plant detritus.
Autumn colours,
Licked by sunlight
Blur around the breakneck chase,
Eight adrenaline-powered paws
Pound the earth,
Finding hard,
Brittle,
Rough
And smooth surfaces
Momentarily ahead,

Momentarily beneath,
Momentarily behind.
Launching from slight heights
And scrambling up mounds
And hummocks,
The pair burst into unfamiliar territory.
Too fast.
The mouse scratches and scrabbles
To rooted safety,
But
The cub falls,
Towards racing water,
Towards angular rocks
And shadowy narrows.
Whoompf!
Gentle jaws snatch scruff
The cub hangs,
Suspended,
And then feels
The lift,
The reversal,
The warmth of her mother's breath.
A flash of tail
And the watching mouse retreats.

Cuttlefish

Come with me
Under weighty waters
To the midnight zone
To the place where you must bring your own colour
Let me illuminate for you in
Every hue

Follow me as I undulate and shoot
Into rock-crevice safety
Silhouette morphing, matching
Hide with me as I blend and disappear

Geese

Inquiring honks	then wings
beat and	running feet
we soar	high in
mild chaos	then unite
fixed tight	in flight
each one	creating lift
our gift	to those
behind us.	Each wing
exactly following	an unseen
undulating ribbon	path through
wet and	dry, cool
and warm	day and
moonlight with	cheering calls.
The leader	tires and
falls back	taking an
assisted place	quickly replaced.
This we	repeat fast
and neat	so each
will lead	taking the
strain, then	retiring
back again.	

Ads

Accommodation wanted

Small herd (of world's largest land animal) looking
for open plains, wooded savannas or forest.
Must be protected from poachers.

Rare pod in search of quiet river location
in area safe from fishing nets.
Unpolluted waters required,
preferably devoid of human habitation.

Unique bale actively looking for quiet
beaches for egg storage.
Seeking areas with no light or traffic pollution.
Undeveloped stretches of sand strongly preferred.

Undersized troop seeking highland forest with active park
guards.
Vast quantities of unpolluted vegetation required
in trap and snare-free area.
Natural landscape views preferred.

Large flutter desperately in search of milkweed meadow for egg
laying.
Land protected from urbanisation
is essential requirement.
Areas free from pesticides also vital.

The Bee

Today, at play, I found a bee
It circled then flew on to me.

It chose to rest upon my shoe
On patterns coloured green and blue.

I saw it clean around its jaws
Then turn its head in thoughtful pause
Foot statue-still, I leant towards.

Pollen dusted every hair
Her sacks bulged with this priceless ware,

Then fine wings beat in sparkly blur
Long legs hung downwards under her.

She rose as if pulled up by string
And met my eyes, there challenging.

A buzz of hope and off she soared
With my words chasing afterwards,

"We'll plant meadows of wildflowers,
We need you in this world of ours."

Today, at play, I found a bee
It spoke in volumes, wordlessly.

Dear Mohammed,

Thank you for your letter,
And for your love of small creatures,
You are right to care so deeply.
Yet, you are wrong on one count,
Splat is not 'just a worm'
He is a hero of the underworld.

Tell your sister that the food she eats
Is nutritious
Because of Splat,
Because he turns nature's litter into nature's fuel.
Tell your sister that Splat prevents floods
By carving out spaces in the earth
For water to run to.

Tell your sister that the skies are filled with
Beautiful, winged beings
Who survive because creatures like Splat
Are fed upon.

Tell your sister that many of our insects are in critical decline
And Splat is as important as a panda or a rhino.
And please feed Splat some flowers from me.

Mother Earth
Aged 4.5 billion

Kennings — Land

Rainforest

    Shade maker
    Weather maintainer
    Cloud conjurer
    Ground stabiliser
    Diversity lover

Cassowary

    Rainforest strutter
    Casque wearer
    Enemy kicker
    'Boom!' maker
    Seed spreader

Kennings — Sea

The Sea

Moon lover
Earth licker
Boat chucker
Pebble thrower
Fish balancer
Sky reflector
Secret keeper

Blue Whale

Surface dipper
Krill lunger
Tail slapper
Barnacle wearer
Depths singer
Wave rider
Record breaker

Kennings — Sky

Sun

>Day bringer
>Plant feeder
>Earth warmer
>Planet conductor
>Life giver

Red Kite

>Thermal rider
>Whistle maker
>Carrion scavenger
>Colour collector
>Woodland nester

When you're done, love, just throw it away

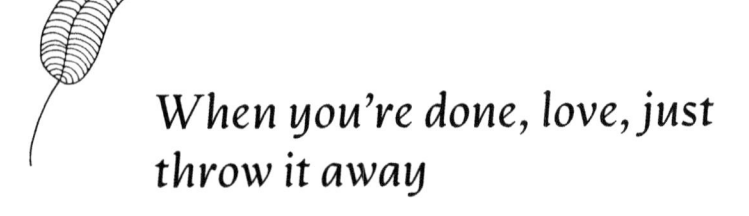

When you're done, love, just throw it away.

Throw it away.

Where is Away?

Who lives there?

I think of all the things I've sent there.

It would fill a room.

Maybe two or three.

And that's just me.

I hope Away is big.

I hope it doesn't mind the smell.

I hope it has a use for all that stuff.

Bowerbird

He collects:

Pen lids

Sweets from kids

Shiny beetles

Knitting needles

Bottle caps

Watch straps

Lost rings

Insect wings

Flower heads

Plastic shreds

Pearly stones

Bits of phones

Foil packets

Metal brackets

Polished springs

Dangly earrings

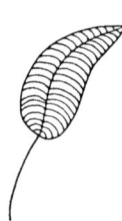

Nearly A Limerick

There once lived a shy axolotl

Who each day placed a plea in a bottle

In the hope it would float

Across the ocean, like a boat

But the poor fool lived in a lake

The Flight of the Last Bee

She soared in an upwards spiral,

Smooth, though off course.

Afraid and alone.

A dusting of pollen was whipped away from her as she fought onwards,

Though she could not find her way.

Something foreign was clouding her senses,

Something stronger than her,

Than them all.

She was losing.
Her buzz dulled

branches of trees appeared to beckon her back,

buttercups raised their beautiful petals, determined to catch one last sight of her,

ut she was gone.

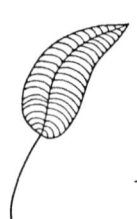

Dear Mother Earth,

Thank you for your letter,
It has made things much better.

My sister won't yet hold Splat,
But I know she gives him peelings,
She doesn't step on bugs now,
And she cares more about my feelings.

I have begun to worry though,
About how long I have Splat for,
I dread the day that's creeping,
When his veggies are untouched,
And he looks as though he's sleeping.

Why can't life go on forever?
Why must all things die?

I wait eagerly and in gratitude for your swift reply.

Mohammed
Aged 7

P.S. Splat is getting very fat!

Life is sweet as a peach on the beach

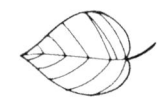

Across the sand
I trace my hand

Over the rocks
I jump without socks

Into the tide
I brace with a stride

Bucket held tight
Terns in flight

In search for a shell
We go for a spell

Then sandy snacks
From greasy packs

And a bite of peach
On this perfect beach

Bucket held tight
Terns in flight

The Pangolin

The pangolin paused,
Paw raised.
Sit
She said without speaking,
But the word was aloud and loud inside me.

Tonight, an animal will visit every child on Earth.
"Why..." I began before the internal whisper-words rushed through me in anticipated answer,
-We are at crisis point and our only hope is to get the young on our side.
"Crisis?" I began and then a wave of scenes hit me like a wall of water...

...Pangolins plucked from lush forest and skinned
...Machines ripping through trees as wildlife screamed
...Islands of waste suffocating sea creatures
...Icebergs cracking
...Forest fires
...Floods
...Disease

Gasping, head in hands, mind racing, I looked to her.
"What can I do? It's too much."
But she had scampered through the window and into the night.
Leaving a small shard of wood behind
With the outline of a pangolin etched into it.

I walked as though in sleep, onto the street
Where every other child had begun to gather,
Each clutching an etched shard,
Orangutan, panther, eagle, moth…

We moved together, clasping hands.
A surge of something magical passed through us.
And we knew
We were the change that was needed.
We would make the difference.

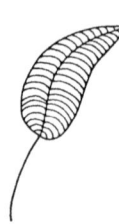

Chameleons

Chameleons

Arbitrarily

Meander through life

Often

Unaware of nearby beauty and dangers

Focused solely on bugs

Lassoing them with sticky tongues, but

Anyone intent on finding one of these

Green (are they?) reptiles

Ends up bewildered

To the hedgehog in my garden

When I first heard you,

I thought the neighbour's cat was ill.

I could not believe you had chosen

Me,

My garden,

To rustle and sniff,

To shovel and scratch.

I watched you,

Nose pressed to steaming window,

Eyes glued,

Heart racing.

You knocked over the den I had built for you,

As you shuffled past on your insect hunt.

I didn't mind,

You found snails,

And made short work of them,

I have the shells in my room,

Along with one of your quills,

I hope that's okay,

It's my greatest treasure.

I watched you until there was no light,

And then I listened,

And in the morning,

I set to work.

I built you a stronger home

With food and water,

And I made you a sign,

It hangs from the cherry tree,

'Spiny's Garden'

What's mine is yours,

My remarkable friend.

The Heavy Hippopotamus

She's a heavy hippopotamus
With heavy hippo feet
Thrashing her heavy hippo head
In the heavy mangrove heat

She's a heavy hippopotamus
With heavy hippo teeth
Sinking her heavy hippo mouth
To the heavy fish beneath

She's a heavy hippopotamus
On the heavy river floor
Much less heavy now submerged
Far more graceful than before.

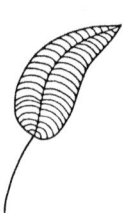

The Crooked Crocodile

He's a crooked, craven crocodile
With crooked spines and claws
With a snatching crooked tail
And a gaping crooked jaw

He's a crooked, craven crocodile
With a crooked, craven mind
Hiding in crooked shadows
With just his crooked form outlined

He's a crooked, craven crocodile
With crooked, craven fears
Lonely in his crooked ways
Crying crooked crocodile tears.

The Worrisome Worm

He's a worn and worried worm
With a worn and worried mind
Wandering worrisome tunnels
Worrying what is close behind.

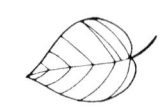

He's a worn and worried worm
With a worn and worried heart
Missing his worn and worried mother
Since they were cruelly torn apart.

He's a worn and worried worm
With a worn and worried tum
But his worried times are over
Because what's behind him, is his mum!

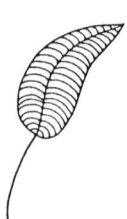

The Ghastly Ghost Bat

She's a ghastly, ghoulish ghost bat
With a ghoulish appetite
Seeking ghastly, ghoulish meals
Not restricted to the night

She's a ghastly ghoulish ghost bat
With ghastly, ghoulish ears
Tuning fast to minute noises
Before the prey even appears

She's a ghastly, ghoulish ghost bat
Patrolling ghoulish shafts and caves
Navigating her surroundings
Using ghastly, ghost sound waves

Dear Mohammed,

You and Splat should feel proud
of the changes in your sister.
Who knows how many others
Will have their environmental compass
Reoriented
Because of this.
One Earth ambassador can lead to many, many more.

Your question is weighty,
And sometimes mere words cannot
Convey
The whole truth, the whole story, the whole picture
But I will try...

When a timer is set upon something
That something has more value,
When we do not know the settings of the timer,
Only that it will run out,
We seek more from each moment,
We value more each choice,
We think deeper,
We love harder...
We are better.

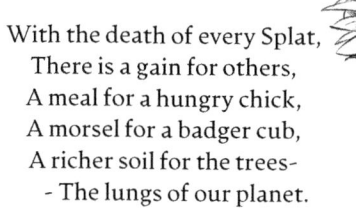

With the death of every Splat,
There is a gain for others,
A meal for a hungry chick,
A morsel for a badger cub,
A richer soil for the trees-
- The lungs of our planet.

Keep asking your questions, Mohammed.

Mother Earth

P.S. Perhaps Splat is not quite what you imagined him to be.

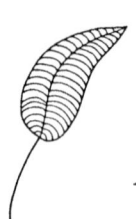

A Symbiosis Love Song

You are the pilot fish to my shark,
The drongo to my meerkat,
The Egyptian plover to my crocodile.

You are the remora to my manta ray,
The pistol shrimp to my goby,
The badger to my coyote.

You are the oxpecker to my rhino,
The clownfish to my anemone
And I love you like a dodder vine loves a nettle.

Snakes

Snakes
love
poems
just
like
kids.
Though
they
rarely
swallow
poetry
whole.
Rather,
they
chew
over
the
meter,
the
imagery
and
syntax.
Then,
digest
it
sl
ow
l
y
.

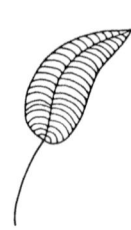

Earth Warrior

Daughter of the Sun
Sister of the Sea
Sand-freckled and
Strawberry-licked

Voice of the breeze
With weather temperament
She grasps elixir in one hand
And sword in the other

Tiger-footed
And tarsier-eyed
The ground moves with her
Noiselessly

Her home is volcanic rocks
Desert dunes
Valley glaciers
and mangrove forest

She breathes with the tide
And sings in bird call
Her heart beats with the winged
She does not sleep

Daughter of the Sun
Sister of the Sea
Sand-freckled and
Strawberry-licked

She is mighty.
She is fearless.

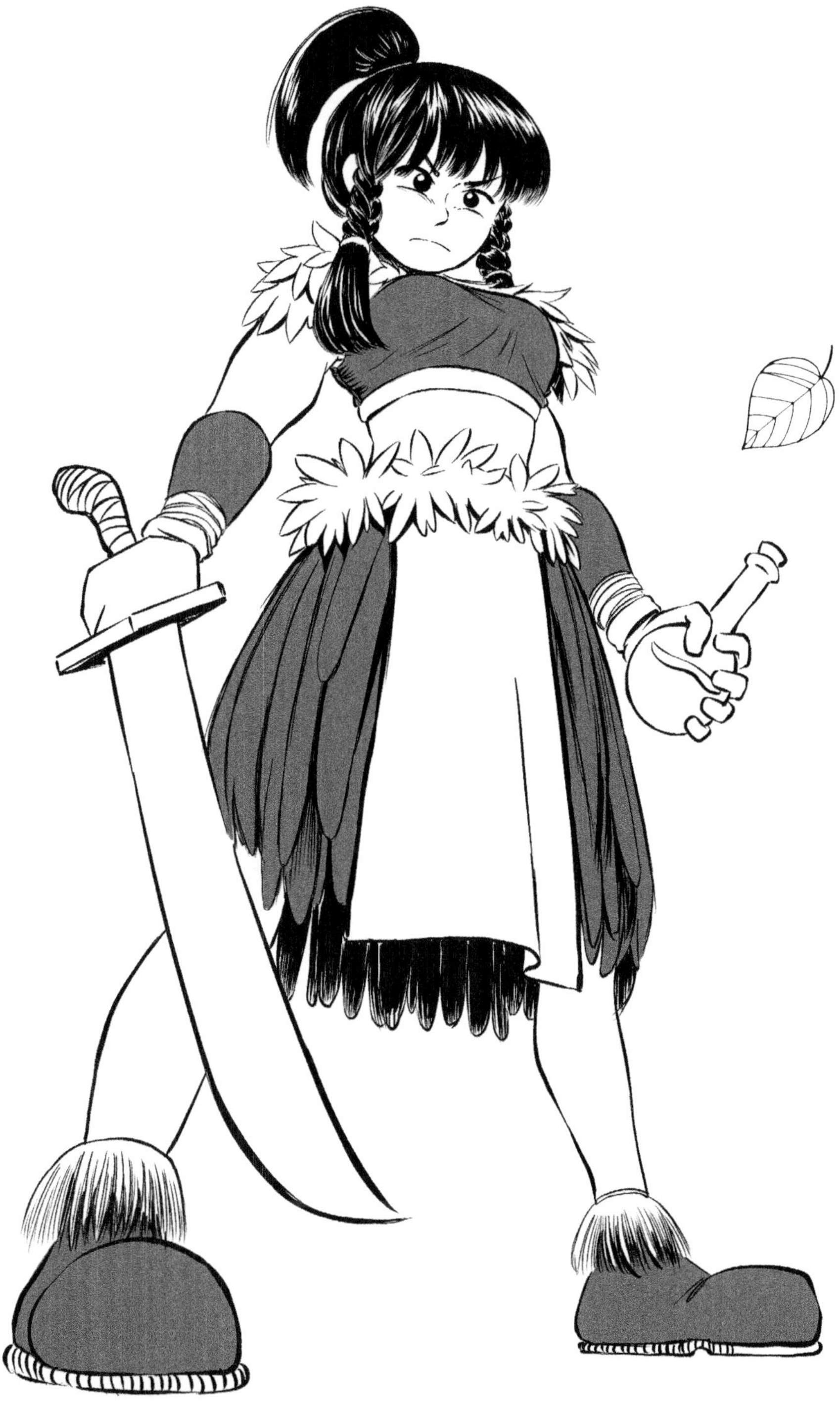

Animal Snacks

Where's the shopping list?
Right in front of you!
But this is just a list of animals...
Let me see that,

> monkey
> kiwi
> fish
> stork
> tiger
> goose
> penguin
> caterpillar

It's folded in half, silly sausage! Look at the other side!

> monkey nuts
> kiwi fruit
> fish fingers
> stork spread
> tiger bread
> goose berries
> penguin biscuits
> caterpillar cake

Nature Bop

Apple pip
Lobster nip
Dolphin flip
Potato Chip

Seal clap
Coyote yap
Carrot snap
Beaver slap

Pea pod
Chicken nod
Amphipod
Hunting cod

Garlic bud
Hippo mud
Rhino thud
Flash flood

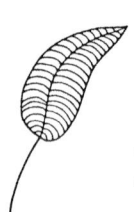

Plunder the ocean

Under the ocean
frisky forms
unruly riot
a world of shell
the thrash of life

Plunder the ocean
frisky forms
unruly riot
a world of shell
the thrash of life

Lessons from mellivora capensis

No species is too large to attack.
(this includes lions)

Feel threatened?
Fire a stink bomb!

Appear to be contained or trapped?
Use those human tools against your captors and escape.

Worried about snake bites?
Just sleep it off.

You can't be eaten with skin this loose,
just twist free of that bite-hold and then bite back!

Hungry? Eat whatever you like.
If it's hiding in a shell, just use your teeth to crack it open.

Want to lull people into a false sense of security around you?
Give yourself a loveable name.......perhaps....... honey badger!

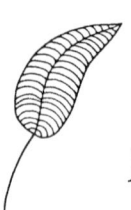

Dear Mother Earth,

Thank you for your words,
I have read them many times,
I hope my timer is a long one,
That I've sought all I can, before it chimes.

This morning, I could not find Splat,
Yet the lid was still in place,
Inaya looked hard too,
We don't know what to do,
So, I turn to you.

Has his timer tolled already?
Has he sunk into the soil?
Did I do something wrong?
I thought he'd grown big and strong.

Sometimes sadness hits me like a wave,
I have that feeling now.
I dwell on all that's wrong on Earth,
The right humans feel they have to plough
Through forest, seas and ground.

Now Splat has gone too.
I don't have faith that he'll be found.

Mohammed
Aged 7 (and a bit)

Haikus

The Ocean
We know so little
Is this the reason we trawl?
To see what was there?

Butterfly
Why are you butter?
Why not marmite or pickle?
Don't settle for bland.

The Shell
The shell in my hand
With its vast untold journeys
In wondrous silence

Is it Okay?
Is it okay that
I could use my pen for change
But instead, doodle?

The Last Koala
Koala with young
Surveying its forest home
Till the last branch falls

Woodlouse
I see your armour
Your fine oval carapace
Nature's transformer

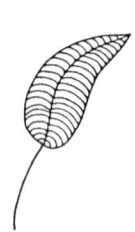

The Crab Apple Tree

The seasons and I are old acquaintances now
We dance our dance
Chase and hide
Call and answer

Winter comes with slow, steady strides
Which harden the ground and provoke the air to bite
My bare branches cast elongated spindly shadows across
Glitter ground

Spring's entrance is playful and spirited
A quick tiptoe, a cartwheel and then she hides
- Is she here? - Or has she slunk away?
She carries her paint pot of fragrant colours
And dabs my branches with pallid pinks and shamrock greens
She fattens and softens my silhouette
And puts out the call to the winged

They come

Summer ushers them too
Lengthening the day for them
Amplifying my colours and warming me to my core
So that the groundwater as it pumps through me
Is an exhilarating rush of cold
The rich shadows cast by my full leaves, now a haven for
Souls in search of cool, earthy shade
Autumn rushes in

She stretches my shadows
A little further each year
She sets fire to my leaves
And they burn for weeks before they fall
When fruit jewels are revealed
Where the flames had been
She lingers like a lifeline
Until the leaf-carpet begins to crisp

Winter is waking

Questions for a whale

When you're in the midnight zone, how can you tell up from down and left from right?

What do you sound like on land?

Do you prefer the sky or the ocean floor?

Questions for an albatross

Do you watch your reflection in the waters below you?

Do you ride on the wind or does the wind fly you?

When you think of the earth, are your thoughts from the clouds?

Sprinklings of blue where no blue normally grew

It became normal
masks marked with tread on the ground
masks gushing from bins
masks caught on branches
floating in puddles
snagged on bushes
and squashed on the roads
blue concertinaed rectangles with white elastic
on every corner
of every street
of every town and city
home and away
too many to count
sprinklings of blue where no blue normally grew
flashes in the flow of the river
- the river
delivering masks in their millions
into the sea
where they float
like diseased jellyfish
tempting turtles, seals, birds and sharks
where they gather
to suffocate coral
where they tangle
trap and torture
where they are transported
to every beach
to every island
inhabited or not
a pandemic

The Egg

Nestled, snug.

Full of potential.

Is it gecko?
Or tern?
Tortoise?
Or platypus?

Is it toothy?
Perhaps feathered?
Furry?
Scaled?

What grows, curled and snuggled within?

Can it feel its brothers and sisters growing alongside?

Does it know that there is a world waiting?
A mother desperate to meet it,
Sunlight, moonlight, earth, sea and stars.

The Sinking of the Ark

The animals went in two by two
But the dingo ate the kangaroo

The animals swept in three by three
Though they swatted at the bumblebee

The animals raced in four by four
A huge heap of droppings piled up on the floor

The animals barged in five by five
So only the hardy had chance to survive

The animals crashed in six by six
Converting the doors to a pile of sticks

The animals leapt in seven by seven
The rams used their horns instead of a weapon

The animals dashed in eight by eight
The lion not divulging what it just ate

The animals shoved in nine by nine
The shocked skunk erupted like a land mine

The animals slammed in ten by ten
And the floor gave way to the water then!

Collective Spell

A cauldron of bats fluttered
Within the shadow of jaguars
As a murder of crows descended.

The quiver of cobras slid close,
Intensifying the cackle of hyenas,
And thus, the charm of finches were released.

Fish

Big fish, small fish
Any size at all fish.
Red fish, blue fish
Any colour'll do fish.

Teethy fish, beaky fish
Hungry for a sneaky fish.
Warm fish, cold fish
Here since years of old fish.

Scared fish, brave fish
Hiding in a cave fish.
Fast fish, quicker fish
See them in a flicker fish.

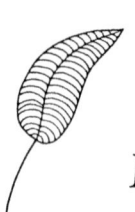

Dear Mohammed,

Perhaps in a different story,
Splat was stepped on at the park.
Be proud of what you gave him,
Of what you achieved together,
And don't lose hope.
Now to wrongs...
I worry too.
But there are many things you can do.
And caring is the most important one.

> *Plant that care deep and firm,*
> *Water it, so on your terms,*
> *It will grow and it will spread,*
> *An ever-branching golden thread*
> *Show it to everyone you know,*
> *Great and small, friend and foe,*

Did you know?

Across the globe
It is the young
Who make the waves of revolution
Who challenge and demand
Who drive others to a better future
Change is coming
If you, and children like you,
Hold on tight to your ideals.

And keep Splat's tank as it is,
For now.

Mother Earth

Strangler Fig

Sticky seedling mislaid inadvertently

Turns epiphyte,

Root devoid at first,

Anchorless, yet ready

Nutrition seeking and leeching,

Gutsy and guileful it grows,

Lengthening skyward and groundward,

Embracing its gigantic tree host,

Racing with relish.

Flash forwards just 20 years,

Its host a hollowing shadow of its former self,

Garroted for soil, water and light.

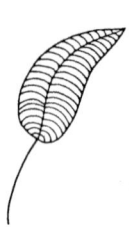

Annual General Meeting of Global Wildlife Representatives

Agenda: Agree on the one invention which should be eradicated from history.

'*Cars*,' piped up the hedgehog from deep beneath the stage,
'*Glass windows*,' declared the gull, barely containing her rage.

'*Pesticides*,' spat the bee, with a lot less buzz than before,
'*Blood sport*,' whispered the vixen, half-tail sweeping low to the floor.

'*Chainsaws*,' asserted the koala with more energy than he could spare,
'*Nets*,' sighed the bluefin tuna from the tank balanced low on a chair.

'*Guns*,' shrieked the orphaned chimp who was rocking back and fore,
'*Fashion*,' sobbed the mink, wiping gathering tears with his paw.

'*Plastic*,' blurted the turtle and the room fell silent and grave,
An imperceptible nod from every face then each paw rose in a wave.

ANNUAL GENERAL MEETING
OF GLOBAL WILDLIFE REPRESENTATIVES

Agenda: Agree on the one invention which should be eradicated from history.

HEDGEHOG	GULL	BEE
CARS	Glass Window	Pesticide

VIXEN	KOALA	BLUEFIN TUNA
Blood Sport	CHAINSAW	NET

ORPHANED CHIMP	MINK	TURTLE
GUNS	FASHION	Plastic

Tankas

The Atacama
Dramatic red rock canyons
Earth's best stargazing
Oldest mummified remains
Now largest fashion landfill

The Great Pacific
Home to orcas, dugongs, seals
To diverse fish life
To the oldest deep ocean,
To trash: thrice the size of France

A Rainbow of Life

Red like the strawberry poison dart frog

Orange like the veined wings of a monarch butterfly

Yellow like the venomous eyelash viper or strange banana slug

Green like the luna moth

Blue like the shining honeycreeper or elusive blue glaucus

Indigo like the purple jewel beetle

Violet like the magnificent sea anemone

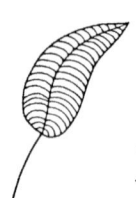

Blackout Poetry — Step 1

...had scarcely thawed. The ground was blanketed <u>in crispy</u>, brittle leaves in a rainbow of <u>autumn colours</u> which glowed vividly in the dappled setting sunlight. They alerted her to <u>its</u> presence. The soft, <u>muted crunch</u> had not been made by her own foot. It had not been made by a human foot. The noise had <u>barely</u> been <u>discernable</u> over the rustling of <u>the last</u> leaves in the <u>trees</u>. It was the step of a <u>stalking</u> creature; the sign of an adept predator. As her legs become unresponsive, her brain fought for a solution. <u>Climbing</u> would not be possible with the lowest of the branches far above arm reach. <u>Fighting</u> would be fatal <u>with no</u> make-shift <u>weapon</u> to hand. She would have to run. <u>Doubtless</u> it could catch her but she needn't run far. Ten metres and she would not be <u>doomed</u> as her legs feared she would. Breathing deep, yet still as...

Blackout Poetry — Step 2

...had scarcely thawed. The ground was blanketed in crispy, brittle leaves in a rainbow of autumn colours which glowed vividly in the dappled setting sunlight. They alerted her to its presence. The soft, muted crunch had not been made by her own foot. It had not been made by a human foot. The noise had barely been discernable over the rustling of the last leaves in the trees. It was the step of a stalking creature; the sign of an adept predator. As her legs become unresponsive, her brain fought for a solution. Climbing would not be possible with the lowest of the branches far above arm reach. Fighting would be fatal with no make-shift weapon to hand. She would have to run. Doubtless it could catch her but she needn't run far. Ten metres and she would not be doomed as her legs feared she would. Breathing deep, yet still as...

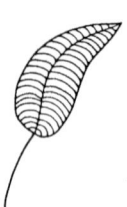

Blackout Poetry — Step 3

The Last Trees

In crispy,

Autumn colours,

Its muted crunch

Barely discernable,

The last trees

Stalking, climbing, fighting,

With no weapon.

Doubtless doomed.

The Assassin

Shelled ninja
Slime-yielding slayer
Kin dispatcher
Cut-throat gastropod

The Assassin Snail

Perchance nature's slowest
Ambush predator

Trailing sluggish prey
In slow-motion chase

Or

Hiding, burrowed below
With syphon bared
Detecting the unsuspecting

Devouring all that is not
Calcium carbonate
And combing for leftovers

Leaving empty shells behind
And slipping quietly away

The Sea

It softens, compresses, sinks and shrinks
the sand,
muddying its colour.

Footprints are rejected, retracted slowly
whilst sandcastles wither
and shells tumble and shift.

Rolling pebbles percuss to the rhythmic, breathy hiss
of its lapping.

It sweeps across sandpiper legs and bills.
They barely register its advance and retreat, in their feeding
trance.

Its timeless, meditative sound cleanses my mind and speaks to
my soul.

A Naturalist's Bookshelf

Out at Sea by I. C. Fish

How to Fight off Bears by Justin Case

Expert Tiger Handling by Claude Body

Riding Waves by Betty Surfs

Exploring Volcanoes by Ivor Hothead

The Mariana Trench by Miles Deep

In a while, Crocodile by Ali Gator

Avalanche Approaching by Luke Out

Birds of the Sea by Albert Ross

Snakes of the Amazon by Anna Conda

The Hypnotic Ways of the Cobra by N Tranced

The Art of Tree Surgery by Tim Burr

Goldfish on the Run by M T Tank

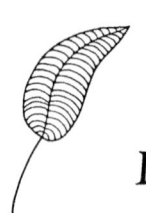

Dear Mother Earth,

Splat had not disappeared!
He'd not died as we had feared.
And he wasn't a worm!

Inaya spotted him emerge
From his cocoon perch,
Tangled in the mossy twigs,
Under flowers, coffee and figs.

He pumped out miraculous wings
Of vivid pink and dazzling gold,
An 'elephant hawk moth', we were told.

We watched him for three hours,
Then his fluttering intensified,
We took him onto the balcony
So, he could be outside.

We clasped each other's hands,
Without saying that we would,
And together, we removed
The lid.

As he fluttered up and out,
He rested briefly on my thumb,
Tears glistened in Inaya's eyes,
And he took off through the skies.

My heart soared with him.
I only wish you could have seen.
That you were with us too.

Mohammed
Aged 7 (and a little bit more)

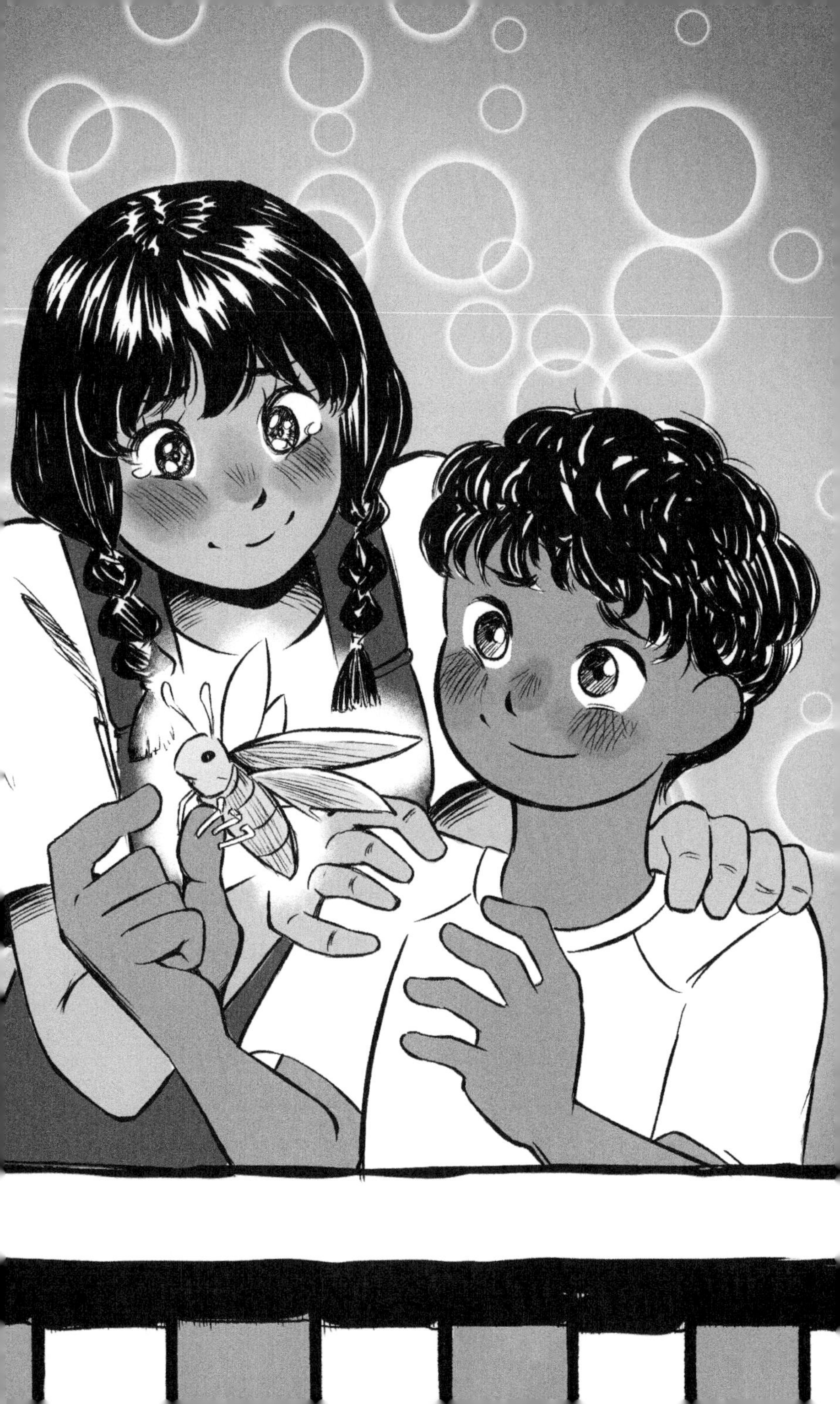

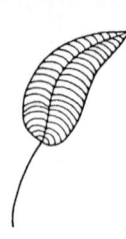

How to infuriate a literary tiger

1. Tie a flaming branch to its tail

    understandably very frightening

2. Confuse it with a lion

    this makes them irrationally angry

3. Give it a tickle

    they are not ticklish, and this is simply an invasion of their private space

4. Invite it to tea

    their teeth are really not designed for cake and biscuits (and tinned tiger food is rank).

5. Read it some Wordsworth

    it greatly prefers the works of William Blake

Take heart, grasp hope: you are mightier than you know

Reduce your flushing
Grow what you eat
Buy what is local
Consume less meat

Find new uses
Champion second-hand
Seek the ethical
Pull heads from sand

Stand firm on beliefs
Walk, cycle and run
Boycott the wasteful
Shrink your footprint to none

Vote for the planet
Challenge and enlist
Be the voice the earth needs
Speak loudly and insist

Take heart, grasp hope:
you are mightier than
     you know!

Weather

Wind
in the wrong place.
Every t i m   e
I try to write poetry in the wind
It blows
o
 f
  f
the page and lands back

Rains
Rains are glorious for poetry
They nourish and re-energise
Washing away all the dirt
Leaving the pearls of wisdom immaculate and exposed
Making the unclear, clear again

Fog
Fog makes it very hard to see where
one line ends and the next
begins but does
that matter
anyway?

A little bird told me

A little bird told me
That a leopard cannot change its spots
That you can't hold with the hare and run with the hounds
That if wishes were horses, beggars would ride.

   It let the cat out of the bag
   And a fish out of water
   It barked up the wrong tree
   Till the cows came home
   It cried havoc and let slip the dogs of war.

      It made a beeline for
      A white elephant
      Like a moth to a flame
      At one fell swoop
      Then it left early to catch a worm.

Volcano

vapour *vapour*
vapour *vapour*

V

io

lent

vase of

vivid lava,

a vibrant valve,

vacant of life and void

of virtue. A vessel of voluminous

voice. A vertical, veritable, veiled villain.

Along came Mungomery

Over in 'stralia, *as many folks say*,
Cane beetles were gorging on tall sugar cane
They fed high on the stalks in the dry heat of day

Along came Mungomery, what a catastrophe!

Cane toads were shipped in to deal with the pest
They were bred and released and set free as a test
But they proved much less useful than their name suggests

Oh Mungomery, what a catastrophe!

The beetles stayed high, and the toads couldn't fly
The toads slept in the day and the ground was too dry
No cane beetles were eaten, and the toads multiplied

Along came Mungomery, what a catastrophe!

The toads soon moved out in search of wet ground
What a feast of prey they very soon found
Small mammals, frogs, reptiles and bugs did abound

Oh Mungomery, what a catastrophe!

The most dreadful results were still yet to come
See, the cane toad is equipped with a deadly weapon
In all its life stages, it exudes toxic venom

Along came Mungomery, a total catastrophe!

A cane toad appears a nice easy bite
To hundreds of species on foraging plight
Who until now have known dangerous prey at first sight

Oh Mungomery, what a catastrophe!

Now cane toads have spread far and they have spread wide
Slaying predators and prey in their continent-sized stride
And few creatures can kill them though many have tried

Along came Mungomery, what a catastrophe!

And to add further insult to this injury-rich tale
A cane toad lays eggs every year without fail
30,000 new hopefuls keen to join the assail

Mungomery, Mungomery, what a catastrophe!

Verae Peculya Names

The sparklemuffin sighed, its springy legs by its side
"People think of unicorns when they hear my name,
especially when it's said, I have a rainbow-coloured head!
How do I explain that I'm a spider instead?"

The clanga clanga nodded, in compassionate accord,
"I too disillusion, causing heartbreak and confusion,
when I'm not a pink space creature with round ears and a trunk!
Though a striking bird of prey with glossy purples on display,
The soup dragon and friends are tricky to debunk!"

"Well, as a cousin of the mako, tiger, bull and megalodon,
I assure you that when they meet me, most think my name's a con!
What creature do you ponder, are you also filled with wonder
when someone utters to you, the name **wobbegong**?"

The wasp surveyed its friends then took its turn to face the lens,
"At least your names are full of marvel, even if they hardly suit,
My name must have been chosen by a real sarcastic brute.
I'm a verae peculya, yes, a verae peculya.
How could one assign this and still remain in good repute?"

The answer is trees

Floods?
　　Plant more trees.

Temperatures rising?
　　Plant more trees.

Habitat destruction?
　　More trees.

Climate change?
　　Trees.

Air pollution?
　　Trees.

Trees. The answer is trees.

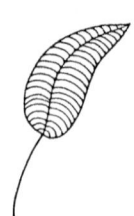

You are welcome here

Taipan,

I see your fangs filled with deadly neurotoxic venom

But you are welcome here

I will leave you be so that you ignore me.

Bull shark,

I watch you enter shallow, brackish waters with teeth bared

But you should swim here

I have no need to enter where you feed.

Crocodile,

I've noted your teeth, your massive gape

But you are free to roam here

I've learned your habits as you would learn mine.

Funnel web spider,

I've witnessed your warning stance,

But your home is here

I will not attack you

        just because I fear you.

Where the Poems Go

Poems sketched on the skeleton of leaves
Nod to the sun then surf on the breeze,

Poems drawn by sticks in the sand
Return to the sea as was always planned,

Poems written in the stars
Shine bright then dim into scattered scars,

Poems scrawled on the mountainside
Erode over time—first they fade then they hide,

Poems floated out to sea
Morph and grow on their fabled journey,

Poems spoken into the night
Merge and converge, diverge and take flight.

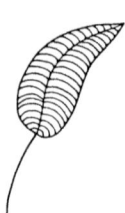

Responsibility: A Reverse Poem

It's not our fault or responsibility

We cannot simply say

Our planet is doomed unless we all change

Our planet has survived for billions of years. Billions! Yet

People throw around misinformation to suit their cause

Coral reefs are dying, extinction is rife, the natural world is gasping for breath

Listen

We need to see the science for what it really tells us

Climate change is a con

So don't shout around that

Humans are selfish, reckless and dangerous

(Now read again from the bottom to the top)

Dear Mohammed,

I saw; I was there.
I am Splat.

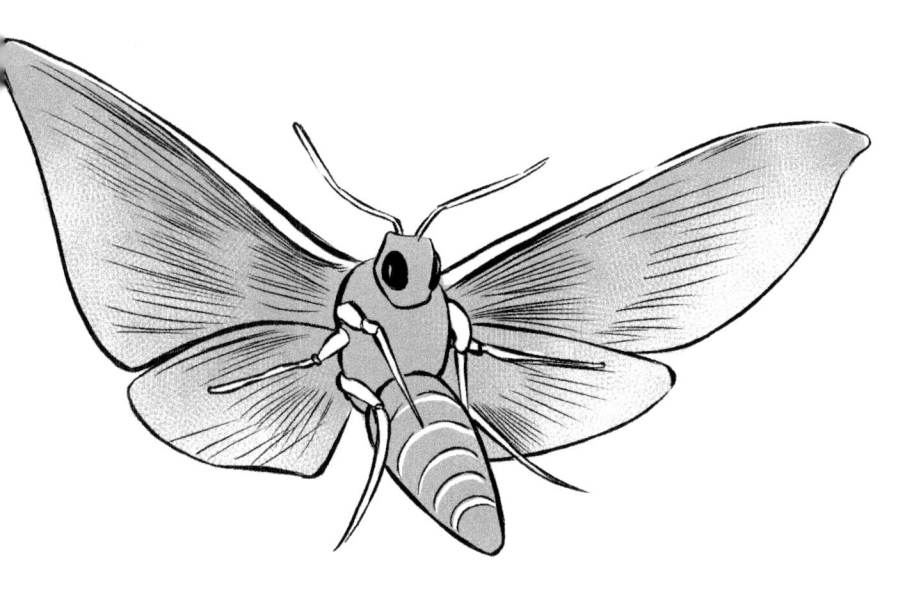

Mother Earth
x

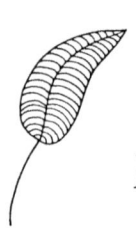

Keep Connected But Not Devices

Keep connected
But not devices
Feel the weather
Taste the air
Plant and water
Dig your share

Keep connected
But not devices
Smell the sea
Study rocks
Notice details
Forget the clocks

Keep connected
But not devices
Forest bathe
Climb the tree
Wade the river
Mind empty

Keep connected
But not devices
Watch our wildlife
Help it thrive
Gorge on joy
Be out and alive

Keep connected
But not devices
Watch the stars
Walk the moors
Beat the sunrise
And then pause
…

Printed in Great Britain
by Amazon